For the People of Chesterfield for ever

A Short History of Queen's Park

Edited by
Janet Murphy

MERTON

A

Published for
The Friends of Queen's Park by
Merton Priory Press Ltd
5 Oliver House, Wain Avenue
Chesterfield S41 0FE

First published 2006

ISBN 1 898937 70 2

Printed by
Higham Press Ltd
New Street,
Shirland,
Alfreton,
Derby DE55 6BP
Tel: 01773 832390

Contents

Preface

This short history of Queen's Park has been produced to mark the restoration of the Park. It includes many memories of events, people and places. Further recollections of cricket will be included in a short history of the game in the Park to be published at a later date.

As editor I would like to thank the people of Chesterfield and beyond who have helped with the production of this booklet. It is dedicated to you all. Please continue to send your memories and photographs to: The Friends of Queen's Park, c/o North Lodge, Queen's Park, Chesterfield S40 2LD.

Recollections of the following have been included here: Mrs J. Baskerville, Clive Baxter, Dianna Bell, John Billyeald, Helen Booker, Betty Booth, Pamela Boult, Stuart Brown, Jean Cockell, Michael Cole, Joan Fenwick, Steve Franks, Christine Gaunt, Roy Goodyear, Tony Hallam, Roger Hartley, Mrs Hoole, Mrs K. Howarth, David Howes, Anne-Marie Knowles, Jack Marsh, Betty Maycock, Janet Murphy, Andy Pashley, Sarah Poulton, John Ramsey, Frank Ramskill, Ken Silcock, Susan Smith, Patricia Southern, Margaret Sowden, Tom Stanton, Mrs A.M. Terry, Colin Wilbourne, Mr Widdowson.

Unless otherwise stated, the illustrations are from my own collection.

Thank you also to Betty Booth, Chesterfield Museum and Art Gallery, Chesterfield Photographic Society, Christine Gaunt, Chris Goodlad, Mrs K. Howarth, George Lowe, Jack Marsh, Carol Morris, Pat Pick, John Smith, Dorothy Wheeldon.

Other people who have helped include Brian Austin, the staff of Chesterfield Library Local Studies and of Chesterfield Museum and Art Gallery, and Lesley Fields *(Derbyshire Times)*.

Thanks for financial support are due to J. and M. Cheetham, Elliot Mather (Solicitors), Eurotec Land Remediation Ltd, Polar Windows and others.

Janet Murphy   September 2006

The Vision, 1887–93

In 1887 the Borough of Chesterfield covered approximately half a square mile. Most of the local industry was outside the boundary of the borough and did not contribute to the rates. Money for essential town improvements was therefore limited.

The poorer inhabitants of Chesterfield lived in cramped, insanitary conditions in the narrow streets around the Market Place. Many of the men spent much of their working day in heavy manufacturing industry or underground in coal mines. Outside working hours there was little for them to do except walk the streets or visit the local inns and beer houses, of which there were over 70. Children had nowhere to play other than the busy market place or the narrow yards around their homes.

In February 1887 a meeting of prominent local inhabitants agreed to commemorate Queen Victoria's Golden Jubilee by raising funds for a public recreation ground for the people of Chesterfield. It was to be six years before their vision became a reality.

There were already two recreation grounds in Chesterfield, both on Saltergate. The Old Recreation Ground, which was used for galas and flower shows, was to the east of the New Recreation Ground, the home of Chesterfield Cricket Club and Chesterfield Football Club. However, the proposed new public recreation ground would be much bigger, could be used by everyone, and the land would belong to the people of Chesterfield, whereas the others were privately owned.

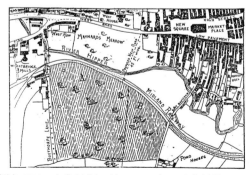

At the time of this map only field A had been purchased, field B was purchased later. Notice the cramped housing between the Market Place and the river, which marked the borough boundary. (T.P.Wood's Almanac 1888)

5

An appeal was launched for £4,250 in order to buy two fields south of the river Hipper, together with a strip of land for a roadway from West Bars. Money was slow to come in but by August sufficient had been promised for the Jubilee Committee to decide to go ahead with the purchase of the larger 17-acre field and the land for the roadway. The field (now occupied by the lake and the open space) cost £3,000.

Consequently Chesterfield celebrated the Queen's Golden Jubilee later than most when, on 21 September 1887, a 'Monster Procession', almost a mile long, wended its way along a circuitous route through the town from the Market Place to a temporary entrance to Queen's Park on Boythorpe Lane (now Boythorpe Road). The Sherwood Rangers provided an escort of cavalry for the 24 drays, representing the trades of the town, and five carriages, carrying the members of the Jubilee Committee. Making up the rest of the procession were school children and members of local friendly societies. A service of dedication was held and a commemorative tree planted. The land was handed to the Corporation for the people of Chesterfield for ever.

An adjacent five-acre field (of which the cricket ground now occupies the major part) was purchased in 1890, almost wholly due to the efforts of the ladies of the town who held a five-day bazaar at the Stephenson Memorial Hall to raise the purchase price of £1,000.

The Jubilee Committee at the dedication ceremony 21 September 1887, the mayor, Alderman T.P. Wood, is in the centre. (Chesterfield Museum)

To produce an income to offset the costs of maintaining the Park, the Council proposed to close it to the public for several days each year in order to charge for skating in the winter, and to rent it out to organisations to hold events such as flower shows and sports. Already the local militia had taken over the original field of the Park for a month in 1888. A year later the Derbyshire Miners' Association held their first annual demonstration in the Park. Demonstrations were non-political; in later years, when the Amalgamated Society of Railway Servants sought to hold a demonstration in connection with the movement for shorter working hours, their application was refused. The land was still rough fields and the Council made money by letting out grazing rights and selling the hay crop.

Although the Local Government Board gave permission for money to be borrowed to pay for laying out the Park, it would not allow the Council to close the Park as it wished, and early plans were abandoned. In 1890 a Public Health Amendment Act was passed, which allowed councils to close parks for up to twelve days a year, and new plans for laying out the Park could be made. The Parks Committee was coming under increasing pressure as there were movements for a shorter working week and half-day closing in the town. The Council offered a premium of £25 for the best design, at a cost of not more than £2,500. William Barron was an eminent landscape gardener who had worked at Elvaston Castle near Derby and designed several parks. Despite his death, aged 85, shortly after the plans were submitted, his was the one chosen; his son oversaw the work.

In March 1892 a mortgage for £2,500 was taken out with the Yorkshire Penny Bank. The Park was closed to the public a month later in order for the landscape contractor, Joseph Tomlinson of Derby, to begin work.

At long last everything was ready and the Corporation exercised its statutory right to close the newly laid out Park to enable the Chesterfield Horticultural Society to hold a flower show on 2 August 1893. More than four thousand people paid for admission and Queen's Park immediately became an important part of town life.

The 1899 flower show, with South Lodge in the background. The young ladies appear to be taking part in a competition for decorated doll's prams. (T.P.Wood's Almanac 1900)

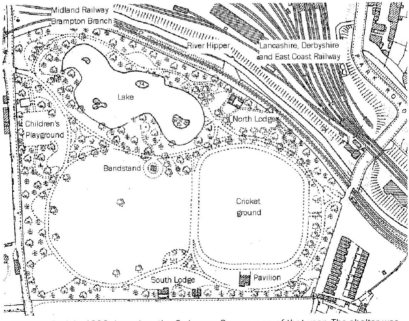

Queen's Park in 1898, based on the Ordnance Survey map of that year. The shelter was later erected on the mound between the bandstand and the lake.

The Golden Years, 1894–1945

The Park was laid out primarily as a recreation ground, where people could take healthy exercise in pleasant surroundings, and where children could play safely. There was a lake, which could be used for boating in the summer and skating in the winter; a gymnasium (swings); a cycle track round the cricket ground; a bowling green; tennis courts and a large open space where children could play football and cricket. The basic layout of cricket ground, open space and lake remains to this day. Of the buildings in the Park today, only North Lodge and the boundary wall were in existence when the Park was opened in 1893.

The original main entrance to the Park was from West Bars by means of a footbridge, over the river Hipper and the Brampton branch of the Midland Railway, at the side of North Lodge, the park keeper's house. A bowling green was laid out adjacent to the house but it soon made way for lawn tennis courts.

There used to be a railway which ran about three or four yards inside the Queen's Park boundary. The railway ran to Robinson's works and branched towards the gas works across the road. It may also have

Recreation Park and Lake, Chesterfield.　　　　Valentine's Series

One of the earliest photographs of the Park showing the original entrance by the side of North Lodge.

Another early photograph, in the distance work on the embankment for the Lancashire, Derbyshire & East Coast Railway is already in progress.

gone to the Brampton Brewery. A chain was drawn across Chatsworth Road to stop the traffic when a train was due. The chain was pulled through a hole in the brick wall on the Gas Works side (1930s). The railway ran at the back of Queen's Park Hotel and crossed the road where there were single level crossing gates. (Stanton)

In 1895 a start was made on the construction of the railway embankment and the Market Place station for the Lancashire, Derbyshire & East Coast Railway. These blocked the main access to the Park. Instead the railway company had to make a new road from the Market Place down Froggatt's Yard and Wheeldon Lane to an entrance in Park Lane (now Park Road). The company also had to provide £500 to build a new cottage in case the original was damaged during construction of the embankment. Instead the Council decided to use the money to repair North Lodge and to build a new South Lodge, which became the park keeper's house. North Lodge was let to a member of the borough police force.

Alderman Edward Eastwood donated the equipment for a gymnasium (mostly swings) which stood on the west side of the Park. Sadly, shortly after the opening, a young girl called Alice Wright was killed when she was struck by a swing occupied by a 'young fellow'. During the inquest considerable surprise was expressed that young

10

The railway is now open. The smoke from the trains must have made the line of washing rather dirty! (Goodlad)

lads were using the swings in a children's playground. The original swings were removed and replaced by some from Lower Brampton School. They were suspended by chains from wooden beams, similar to those in the junior area today. By 1903 a separate playground was in existence for girls. In the early years, the park keeper was instructed to lock the swings on a Sunday to prevent their use.

The mayor, Alderman T.P. Wood, was made a Freeman of the Borough of Chesterfield for his services as chairman of the Jubilee Committee. Instead of a silver casket to hold the scroll, he requested that the money be used to establish a fund for a bandstand. This wooden structure stood by the lake and the cricket ground and Chesterfield Volunteer Band played there at the opening flower show. In 1906 the Park Orchestra was asked to refrain from playing selections from comic operas on a Sunday afternoon!

Another necessity in the Park was a shelter in case of inclement weather. Again funds were raised by public subscription and the shelter opened in 1902 as a memorial to the three years during which Alderman Spooner served as mayor. It is sometimes referred to as the dove house.

The shelter remains today, but the bandstand was demolished in 1919.

Chesterfield Football Club was formed in 1867 by members of the Cricket Club who wanted to keep fit during the winter. In 1893 the two clubs were sharing the New Recreation Ground, Saltergate, hardly an ideal situation. The Cricket Club decided to move to the Park and the first match was played there in 1894. The pavilion came from the Old Recreation Ground.

The cricket ground was laid out to a high standard with the idea that county sides might play there. In 1897 Chesterfield Cricket Club applied for permission to organise a first class match the following season and offered to prepare the wicket. The old pavilion was replaced by a larger one in time for the first county cricket match in the Park in 1898. Although the ground was, and still is, the home of Chesterfield Cricket Club, other local clubs such as Robinson's Wheatbridge Works, the Borough Police and local tradesmen have played there. Chesterfield Cricket Club continued to employ a seasonal groundsman to maintain the ground. In 1904 W.G. Grace made his second appearance on the ground, playing for London County. The same year there was a most remarkable cricket match.

I sat next to a retired gentleman, who was in his eighties ... The most important memory he had, and conveyed to me, was that he had been a Derbyshire supporter all his life and he had been present at the first match in the Park in 1898 when Derbyshire played

The pavilion of 1898. The gables at either end were raised at a later date to make rooms on the upper floor.

Surrey. He said that at the time the pavilion was just the bit in the middle, the two gable end portions were added later. In 1904, which caused a few headlines, Essex batted first and scored 597 with Perrin making 343 not out. Derbyshire batted and reached 548 before lunch on the third and final day and a draw appeared likely. However Essex were dismissed for 97 and Derbyshire required 147 to win in just 125 minutes. They reached the total with 45 minutes to spare. The retired gentleman had been there and it was his greatest memory of the Park. (Silcock)

The pavilion also served as a grandstand for events in the Park. In 1893 a Mr Cole was permitted to serve refreshments from a table on the side of the road from West Bars. Once the new pavilion was built, refreshments were served there.

Athletics and cycling events had been important since the Park was opened. Evening sports were held by the Chesterfield Cycling and Athletics Club and, in the early days, by the Cricket Club. Cycling and athletics events formed part of other events such as the flower show. The events were of a high standard. In 1896 the captain of Chesterfield Cycling Club was Thomas Jebson Gasgoyne, the World Amateur Cycling Champion for that year.

Evidently a large committee was needed to organise the evening sports.

From the start, events in the Park were hugely popular and, in 1900, a terrace was built to the west of the pavilion and seating provided — planks of wood on iron supports. The same year 6,500 children were entertained in the Park to celebrate the relief of

The men had their own fashion parade at this early flower show, about 1905.

Mafeking. Other events attracting large crowds were the festivities for the coronation of Edward VII, Empire Day celebrations and military parades.

The flower show of the Chesterfield and District Horticultural Society was held annually. One of the most successful shows was held in 1905. There were classes for nurserymen, professional gardeners, amateurs and cottagers. The Chesterfield Volunteer Band played selections throughout the day. In the afternoon there were heats of athletic and cycling events. Before the finals, there was a balloon ascent, something of a novelty, and last of all a firework display. The balloon was filled with coal gas and it drifted as far as Rotherham. In 1906 the gas was damp, and therefore heavy, and the balloon failed to leave the ground. Another successful attempt with a smaller balloon was made in 1907, but that was the last. The chief aeronaut was Eustace Short, one of the Short Brothers (aircraft manufacturers), who had worked briefly in the Borough Engineer's Department.

'The balloon that would not go' in 1906. (Chesterfield Museum)

An early Sunday school demonstration, by North Lodge.

Another event with almost as long a history was the annual demonstration by the Sunday School Union on Whit Monday. The first to finish with a service in the Park was in 1903. In later years decorated floats were added to the procession.

Thought to be scholars from the Ragged School, about 1925. (Wheeldon)

One memory I have of the Whit Walk was that when it was over, we were given an orange and a teacake each. I enjoyed the orange, but I clearly remember eating the fruit out of the teacakes and feeding the rest to the ducks. (Booth)

Some times there were a couple of fruit stalls selling their wares. I think it was in those days when the Whit Walk was on Whitsuntide. (Maycock)

The original idea for a recreation ground did not come from Alderman Wood, but without his leadership the scheme might well have not been carried out. He was also the driving force behind the purchase of additional land to extend the Park as a memorial to the reign of Queen Victoria, following her death in 1901. The land was formally handed to the Council in 1905. Possibly because there was already a wall round the Park the 'Annexe' was never incorporated into the Park, instead it was surrounded by 'unclimbable railings'.

During the First World War most able-bodied men went into the Forces and there was only a small military presence in the town. Without members, the cricket and tennis clubs ceased to function, although cricket matches were held to raise funds for the British Red Cross. There were band concerts in aid of the Mayor's Relief Fund and by the Royal Marine Band on behalf of the fund for providing comforts for the Navy. The Local Volunteer Defence Corps held a review and the 2nd Battalion of the Derbyshire Volunteers was inspected.

There were big crowds for the celebrations to mark the end of the First World War on Peace Day, 19 July 1919. A grand military procession with representatives of the Armed Forces, including the women's services and Voluntary Aid Detachments, made its way from the Recreation Ground on Saltergate. The procession was accompanied by three bands and there was a fourth band playing selections in the Park. The Grand Military Athletics Sports in the afternoon included a pillow fight and a 'Yards for Years Race'. On the Sunday there was a Grand Music Festival with a choir of 500 singers accompanied by massed bands and an orchestra.

An unexpected consequence of the war was the arrival of a tank in the Park in recognition of the efforts made by the town in raising war savings.

After the Great War, cities and towns, depending upon what they contributed towards the war effort, were awarded items of military history etc. Chesterfield got a tank and two guns. The two guns

The massed choirs on the terrace at the side of the pavilion on the occasion of the concert to celebrate Peace Day July 1919. (Wheeldon)

were positioned on Ashgate Road adjacent to the Drill Hall either side of the main entrance. The tank was placed in the Park near the lake. To get it into position a large part of the perimeter brickwork had to be removed on the corner of Boythorpe Road and Boythorpe Avenue.* Years afterwards it was possible to see where the repair had been effected, there were different bricks and it did not match up. (Silcock)

During the restoration, when repointing was being done on the wall at this point, the wall was found to be in imminent danger of collapse. (Ramsey)

The guns were in fact purchased from the War Office in 1910. They stood with the tank on the site of the original bandstand until 1931 when it was proposed to move them all to the Drill Hall on Ashgate Road. As the estimated cost of this operation was £150, possibly only the guns were moved and the tank was sold as scrap, the proceeds going to the Borough Welfare Fund, the British Legion and the Royal Hospital.

* Boythorpe Avenue had not yet been built but there was a footpath along the wall.

18

During the First World War little maintenance of the bandstand was possible and the structure became so dangerous that it was demolished in 1919 and the site levelled. A temporary bandstand was erected which was transferred to Brearley Park when a new one was built on the present site in 1922.

About the same time the construction of Boythorpe Avenue separated the Park and the Annexe. A new entrance was made from Boythorpe Avenue and in 1926 wrought iron entrance gates were installed. The wooden gates on Park Road and Boythorpe Road were replaced seven years later.

After the First World War a Sports Committee was formed to promote sport across the borough and to develop the Park Annexe. The Parks Committee was responsible for allocating and maintaining areas in the parks and recreation grounds for sporting activities which they then rented out to the Sports Committee. Needless to say there was much confusion, with the Cricket Club applying to both committees for permission to arrange a county match. Some councillors served on both committees and it is difficult to see why the Sports Committee was responsible for arranging band concerts. After much discussion, plans to erect a stadium in the Annexe for the town football club came to nothing, and in 1925 the Sports

The tank and its accompanying guns on the site of the original bandstand.

Gymnastic displays were popular at events until the 1930s.

Committee became a sub-committee of the Parks Committee. Part of the open space in the Park had been used for football, which was now transferred to the Annexe. Cycling and athletics remained popular. The Cycling and Athletics Club organised the Derbyshire Times walk which finished in the Park from 1926.

There was great excitement for local children in the early thirties.

The children's playground was where the leisure centre is now. Boy's and girl's swings were divided by a corrugated iron partition. Around 1930 this was removed, a slide brought in and a roundabout. The queue for a turn was almost to the bottom of Boythorpe Road. (Booth)

An abiding memory is of my older brother taking me to the Park and getting me on a roundabout — the witch's hat I believe it was called. Faster and faster it went round until I was violently sick. Barrie vowed never to take me again. I remember being taken by my elder sister, who was of course more gentle than big brother. We listened to the band and she taught me how to make the swing 'go' by moving my legs in and out in the effective rhythm. I loved to slide head first down the big gleaming slide and when my own mother or the mother of a friend took a group of us to the Park we would form a 'snake' to slide down together. We thought it would be faster that way. One lunch time when I would be about 5 or 6 years old, a playmate and I slipped out of school to go to her home for a mug of sweet tea and we decided to stop at the Park on the way back to school. When we did arrive at school the gates were locked. We shook the gates and

20

called out to our teachers — we could see our classmates doing PE in the playground. No one heard us, so we went back to the Park, playing there till dusk — this being in the height of summer! (Bell)

The swings were behind high hedges, there were swings, a slide, a big one, we used to put candle wax on it to make it go faster when we came down it, a bobby's hat, that was a roundabout in the shape of a bobby's hat, a spider roundabout, and a see saw. Outside the swings area there was a water fountain where we could have a drink of water. (Maycock)

Just through the Boythorpe Road entrance and adjacent to the lake was the water fountain and we used to go there and press the plier-like grip of handle for the water to squirt up into our mouths. The fountain had been presented to the Park by the Chesterfield Sunday School Union. (Silcock)

In his annual report to the Parks Committee in 1932, the Parks Superintendent, Mr McIntosh, said: 'It is gratifying to report that the Children's Playgrounds in the various Parks and Recreation Grounds

continue to be a great attraction to the children, and have been the means of providing them with many hours of enjoyment safe from the dangers of road traffic.' Not everyone liked the sound of children enjoying themselves. In 1936 the Parks Committee received a petition from the residents of Boythorpe Road asking for the swings to be removed. The committee decided to take no action.

One child remains famous long after her death. In the conservatory stands the statue of a child, finger on lips, hiding a rose behind her back.

The drinking fountain installed 17 April 1935 by the Chesterfield and District Sunday School Union with the Revd Dr Townley Ward, the Union's national president. (Chesterfield Museum)

The little girl is Alice Evelyn Sybil Lee, later nicknamed Lalla. She was very fond of roses and one day was unable to resist picking a

The newly carved statue of Lalla in the garden at Dark Lane (Morris)

bloom from her father's favourite bush. At that moment, she heard a footstep and, guiltily hiding the rose behind her back, finger to her lips, she turned to see her father, Herbert Lee, approaching. He was a master builder, stone mason, accomplished carver and sculptor of note, and he told her to stay just like that and immediately began carving into the nearest lump of stone, the gate post of their garden in Dark Lane, now Peveril Road. Three-year-old Lalla's punishment was to take up and hold that pose many times over the coming days until the statue was complete. For some time the statue stood in the family garden, attracting much interest and favourable comment from passers by. Then Herbert was approached by two friends, fellow masons, who coveted the lovely artwork. His way out of the dilemma was to gift the statue to the Borough Council, on February 23rd 1909, stipulating that it should stand in Queen's Park in perpetuity. For many years, the statue overlooked the cricket pitch, much to Lalla's amusement as cricket was a game she disliked. (Dianna Bell — Lalla's daughter)

The lake was also very popular.

22

I remember going 'fishing' in the lake with net and jam jar. We pushed through the bushes near the entrance on Boythorpe Road where a stone slab stood over a water inlet into the lake. Hours were spent catching 'Bullyheads' and such like. We must have shortened their lives quite drastically. (Booth)

The boats on the lake were always an attraction. You could go out for half an hour, possibly 6d. a trip. The main motor boat was painted cream and green and was named Queen Mary. There was a large family rowing boat, called Muriel, which had a rudder, it took two people to row it. The boatman in charge would do his nut shouting: 'Come in no 6' etc. and blowing his whistle. (Silcock)

The friendly boat-keeper called Wilf always made sure we were safe and sound on the lake, anyone causing problems was given the whistle, this meant Wilf blowing his whistle like mad at you, meaning that you had to come off the boats in shame, this was the last thing you wanted, therefore you behaved yourself, so peace was the order of the day. (Southern)

The lady on the right is Miss Annie Bocock. The two gentlemen are her brother, who was killed during the First World War, and her cousin. (Wheeldon)

The motor boat caught fire in 1961 and it was replaced by a landing craft with an outboard motor. This ran for some years until safety considerations banned rowing boats and a motor boat on the lake at the same time. (Ramskill)

The lake was also used for sailing [model] boats. The idea was to place the boat in the water, watch it sail through 360degrees and all have a good time. On this occasion we placed the yacht on the lake, away it went into the middle of the lake and stopped, no wind, no nothing and the rowing boats were not in operation as it was 'out of season'. Desperation set in as we waited and waited; visions of having to go home to Dad, lost yacht – possibly another good hiding? After about an hour the wind freshened and the yacht started to drift towards the summerhouse opposite. Anyway it gradually approached shore and a young lad with a bamboo fishing net let me borrow it. Eventually with one of my pals holding onto me, we managed to retrieve the yacht and bring it ashore. Needless to say we never went yachting again and later on doing schoolboy swaps I exchanged it for something else. (Silcock)

The winter months in those days were quite severe, winter was winter, the lake used to be frozen over and when it was safe to skate or make slides on it we did, other people used to be on the frozen lake as well. (Maycock)

The lake was a big attraction for children

Few of the 'skaters' appear to have skates as they pose for the cameraman. (Chesterfield Museum)

On one occasion I can remember the lake freezing over, and it was interesting to watch people skating around on it. (Southern)

My favourite memory of Queen's Park is walking on the frozen lake in the winter of 1947, holding firmly on to my mother's hand. (Brown)

One winter's day when my mother was about five years old she went to the Park with her brother who was two years older. The lake was frozen, so mum decided to slide on the ice, not realising that the ice was not firm enough and in she went. Fortunately a lady and gentleman were walking by the lake and came to mum's rescue. The lady took off her fur coat and wrapped mum in it. These two good Samaritans took mum and her brother home to Foljambe Road. (Gaunt)

We used to watch a little old man, all dressed in black, skating. He was very good, but we thought he was a spy. (Sowden)

At the western end of the lake a paddling pool was opened in 1934.

The children's paddling pool was great fun on hot days, where we could cool off. (Southern)

As you went left through this gate [Boythorpe Road] you came to 'The Paddling Pool'. This was an oval affair. You went down two small steps into a concrete pool with water about a foot deep. (Booth)

It was situated on the side of the lake, opposite the last island on the lake, near the Boythorpe Road entrance and adjacent to the

25

Chesterfield and Brampton railway line. It was crescent shaped, possibly 20 yards long and five or 10 yards wide. It had a step at each end and on its edge a concrete wall about 12 inches in height. Water ran in from the Boythorpe Road end and filtered out into the lake near the boating lake entrance. We went to the paddling pool and started paddling. Of course Ken 'Big Head' Silcock had to be clever and show not only the Pearson family but the rest of the visitors how good I was. I have not changed. I stood on the concrete wall to show my mastery and slipped and fell right into the paddling pool, getting thoroughly wet through and egg all over my face in the process. In this bedraggled state I was taken home by Betty Pearman. (Silcock)

He was not the only one; several others fell in the paddling pool or the lake.

One day a gentleman climbed the chestnut tree for conkers and fell into the water. (Booth)

When I was six years old I was at the Park with my mum and some friends. I loved to feed the ducks and this particular day I ventured too close to the water's edge and fell into the lake. I can clearly remember my mum pulling me out and trying to dry me off. Fortunately it was a hot sunny day. (Booker)

I remember falling in the lake on my 5th birthday in April 1960. I was rescued by a gentleman, and I remember waving an umbrella in the air, it was a birthday gift. I also remember being taken to a clothes shop, Cheapside, I think it was, where the Ashgate Hospice shop is now, for a new dry outfit. We used to go to the Park a lot when my brothers and I were young. (Terry)

For one boy it was an embarrassing experience.

There was an embarrassing moment associated with the children's paddling pool on the town side of the lake, just along from the landing stage for the rowing boats. I had been taken by a neighbour and her daughter for a picnic and day's amusement at the pool. I lost my footing and, wearing not swimming trunks but short trousers, got a complete soaking. I had to suffer the indignity of returning home in a spare pair of girl's knickers. (Hallam)

For some the episode was more traumatic.

My father's stepbrother took him to the Park in a pushchair. It would be between 1910 and 1918. At that time the lake had large stones on the edge. The pushchair hit one of the stones so hard that my father was catapulted into the lake. He went under and came up with blood pouring from his forehead, where he had cut it. He carried the scar for the rest of his life. (Howes)

The lake was also home to a variety of water fowl.

We had two black swans which never bred because a white male swan kept attacking them. One very cold winter the black male was so stressed that he was unable to preen himself; water was freezing on his wings and the weight was dragging him under the water. The rangers carried the pair to a shed in the Park, where they were nursed back to health. They were then taken to some water at Barlow where they bred. At different times we had bar-headed geese, Muscovy ducks that liked to sit in the sun, mandarin ducks and pochard. They all disappeared, some of them went off down the river. We also had an Indian Runner duck which had an aversion to water. It used to go grubbing around in the dirt and got dirtier and dirtier. At one time we had some bantams and a cockerel along the cycle track. We also had a terrapin which used to sun itself. (Pashley)

He [the park keeper] knew some of the ducks, he called them by name, a muscovy duck was called Charlie. We used to take a slice of bread, break it up and shout the ducks' names and they used to come to us. Every day a man from the Co-operative bakery across

The boat house can be seen across the lake

27

the road in Boythorpe Road used to bring a sack of broken buns, tarts, bread for the ducks and the swans in the park, there used to be different ducks in the Park in those days. Anyway the man used to put it on the side of the lake for the livestock to eat. (Maycock)

At one time there were five swans, but the numbers dwindled to two. When one of those died, the other died of a broken heart. (Ramskill)

At different times aviaries were built but they did not last long.

At the side of the dove house there was an aviary or pets corner, where there were golden pheasants, peacocks and peahens, and a few other birds. They were very interesting as we had not seen any birds like them. After a few years, they kept being vandalised so they were taken away and the aviary dismantled. (Maycock)

Does anyone remember the mynah bird in the aviary near the lake at the bottom of the bridge and probably guinea pigs? (Hoole)

Keeping order were the Parks Superintendent and his staff. North Lodge was occupied by a member of the police force until 1924. It was then occupied by a member of the park staff until 1939, when it was turned into offices. To indicate their authority members of the staff were issued with uniforms.

The Island and Pigeon House, Chesterfield

The pigeon house — this somewhat unstable looking structure did not last long. It was soon lowered to ground level and disappeared, possibly when the shelter was opened in 1902.

28

There used to be a park keeper, he used to open the Park, then at night he either blew a whistle or rang a bell to tell you it was closing, and either walked or cycled round the Park to make sure all the people were out so he could lock the gates. (Maycock)

A bell was rung 15 minutes before the gates were locked. I remember being locked in the Park and having to go to South Lodge to ask the park keeper to let us out of the door into Boythorpe Avenue. It was dark and quite scary. (Booth)

It used to take an hour to close all the gates and make sure that everyone was out of the Park. (Ramskill)

The Park always had a ranger suitably attired — black C.B.C. uniform with a flat hat, with 'PARK RANGER' inscribed on it in gold lettering. The last one really of this era was Cyril but I cannot remember his surname. He lived on Maynard Road — a really nice chap. He used to patrol during daylight hours seeing that all the visitors obeyed the by-laws displayed on the three large boards situated at the entrances on Boythorpe Road, Park Road and Boythorpe Avenue. The signature at the bottom was Mr J.E. Tindale, Park Superintendent, and a slot opening stating that the park closes today at — . Also a notice stating that the closing bell would be rung to enable all visitors to leave the Park in time. I cannot remember if it was 15 or 30 minutes before actual closing time. We never knew which gate would close first. The actual closing bell was situated on the chimney of the greenhouse situated on Boythorpe Avenue. The employees had their entrance in that wall. We always had to dash to ensure we did not get locked in. Some did and had to leave through the employees' entrance. The South Lodge was occupied by the Boothby family. Mr Boothby was the Deputy Park Superintendent. (Silcock)

The first glasshouses were erected in the Park in 1897, and the park keeper was authorised to purchase 2,000 plant pots for plant propagation for the displays in the Park and elsewhere. There were additional greenhouses at Tapton House after the estate was given to the town by Charles Markham. In 1920 the chairman of the Parks Committee, his vice-chairman and the park keeper went to Chatsworth with a view to purchasing a boiler and spare glass to use in the Park, and came back with a large greenhouse! The greenhouses were not open to the public but in 1930 a conservatory was purchased where they could inspect the displays.

Some idea of the scale of operations comes from the report of the Parks Superintendent, Mr McIntosh, in April 1932: 'Approximately 25,000 summer flowering plants were propagated in Queen's Park for the embellishment of the flower beds and borders in various parks and open spaces ... The border of dahlias in the Queen's Park provided a most attractive feature. A display of flowering and foliage plants was maintained in the Conservatory at the Queen's Park throughout the year ... 300 trees and shrubs were planted out.'

Band concerts remained popular, and by the 1930s there were as many as 30 each season, including two by concertina bands.

The Borough Police also held athletics events and a gala. In 1934 the spectators were treated to displays from mine rescue teams and the local fire brigade, with its new Leyland fire engine. A leaking hose soaked a section of the crowd and a wayward hose sprayed the mayor and several members of the council!

Flower shows continued until 1934 when a drought during the summer, a storm on the second morning, and rain on the final evening, 'conspired to make the plants, flowers and vegetables the poorest and the attendance lowest for several years'. The society incurred a substantial loss and the event was not repeated

The herbaceous border, opposite South Lodge, in the 1930s.
The town skyline is still visible.

The Park, Chesterfield.

A band concert in the original bandstand.

The conservatory in the 1980s.

The Northern Counties Athletics Association Centenary. The two boys are Kevin and Andrew Howarth, the nephews of John Billyeald, who designed and executed the design (Howarth).

The toddler's playground near the cricket ground in the late 1980s.

An autumnal scene near North Lodge (Booth).

A familiar view, but extreme weather in the late 1960s (Pick).

A concert in the newly restored bandstand.

Near the Leisure Centre, this flower bed with perennial planting is on the site of the Edgar Styler rose garden (Smith).

although, in the mid 1960s, there were flower and vegetable shows organised by the Chesterfield and District Allotment Council on August Bank Holiday Monday.

The last Sunday school procession to finish in the Park was in 1934 when there were 2,000 scholars, 400 teachers and 20 decorated floats in the procession. Unfortunately the following year the weather was atrocious, the tableaux could not be paraded, and the procession finished in the Market Place. The demonstration continues to this day but not in the Park.

The annual carnival, organised by the Chesterfield Royal Hospital Voluntary Workers Association, was the latest in a long line of events held in the Park to raise money for the Chesterfield and North Derbyshire Royal Hospital. Initially these were days organised by friendly societies but the carnival was a week-long affair.

Fancy dress and floats through the town to the Park, each year until 1939, every August. Ceased because of the war and never revived. (Wilbourne)

Processions used to come out of town and into the Park through the Park Road entrance. I can remember lanterns lit and hanging in the trees, and thinking what a lovely sight. Also ladies dressed up, performing in choirs and giving concerts etc. (Silcock)

Each year Chesterfield had a carnival. The funds raised were for the Royal Hospital. The parade started somewhere on Saltergate. I remember being at the top of Foljambe Road and walking amongst a lot of people in fancy dress. We all finished in Queen's Park where all kinds of stalls and events carried on into the evening. This was the culmination of a week of happenings: dances and talent shows etc. I remember during one of the Carnival weeks the Carnival Queen and her six attendants were in a float that resembled a glass-sided bus decked out with palms etc. They were all desperate to go to the toilet so my grandmother, who was acting as chaperone, suggested they drove round to Boythorpe Road to go to our toilet. Later in the day, when my dad came home from work and heard what had happened, he chalked 'Patronised by Royalty' on the loo door (they were outside in those days). (Booth)

The evening sports held to raise funds for the hospital were very popular.

A Spire Road Club cycle race in the 1930s. (Chesterfield Museum)

The councillor responsible for this for many years was Alderman T. J. Mitchell. The sports included track and field events and cycling and different amusing games etc. One highlight was the 'errand lads' race. One errand lad from each business or shop in Chesterfield was invited to compete on their shop bikes. My brother won the race in 1935. He worked for Unwins the butchers in lower Market Hall on Low Pavement. My brother says that they had to travel one circuit of the track starting at the left side of the pavilion seating just opposite the path to the conservatory. The white line on the tarmac was there for many years afterwards. After travelling one circuit, the finishing tape was opposite the cricket pavilion. Ironically, the prize was presented by Unwins for this event and it was a joint of beef. Anyway it caused a laugh in the Silcock household. My Dad was pleased because we would be at least 2s. to 2s. 6d. better off that week. My brother took part in other races, riding his 'Hetchins' racing cycle. It cost £14 — a lot of money in 1937/8. In 1938, when he was riding, one of the riders came off causing a pile-up, which my brother could not avoid. He was taken to the Chesterfield Royal Hospital. David Dickenson brought my brother's bike home, my mother was quite worried. Eventually my brother came home in an ambulance, the worse for wear. My Dad was not pleased, he had to pay 5s. for the ambulance and he told my brother not to come off again. One lad in the egg and spoon race stuck the egg on the spoon with chewing gum. When he won *and was discovered, he was immediately disqualified, the prize going to the second cyclist. One highlight was the 'He'll take the High Road' cycle race. This consisted of 12 riders doing 12 laps of the cycle track. The last rider on the first lap fell out, the next last on the second lap and so on until the final three laps when the last three riders had to race it out. My brother said that it caused some very exciting races, and much spectator interest, although he was never strong enough to actually win the event. (Silcock)*

1935 George V and Queen Mary Jubilee Celebration. Attractions in the Park included pillow fights on a greasy pole, also a tug of war. (Wilbourne)

Big crowds came to watch the county cricket matches particularly during the glory years of the 1930s. Derbyshire won the championship in 1936, and in the same year the first cricket festival was held at Chesterfield.

During the Second World War there was a big military presence in and around the town and men in reserved occupations were less likely to be conscripted than they would have been during the First World War. The Park Annexe was requisitioned by the military for a drill ground and later for accommodation. The bowls and tennis facilities remained in use, although the public had to share them with the Services. The Queen's Park Tennis Club continued to use

A council team in July 1930. The notice 'Autographs prohibited' was probably left over from the visit of the Australian touring team two months earlier. (Chesterfield Museum)

the hard courts in the Park throughout the war, but the activities of Chesterfield Cricket Club were severely curtailed.

> *Chesterfield Cricket Club shared their ground with Chesterfield Tube Works during the war, the Tube Works ground being out of commission, also some time during this period the Royal Engineers played there, being stationed at the Boythorpe Drill Hall. There were celebrity matches played between G.H. Pope's XI v Mayor's XI when famous international players appeared.* (Wilbourne)

> *During the 1940s soldiers used to bring their girl friends, or come to get a girl friend. It used to be packed, everyone used the Park. I think the soldiers used to come from the Queen's Park Annexe, as it used to be an army camp during the war.* (Maycock)

> *As a teenager, I learned to row a boat on the lake. I met my late husband who was stationed in Clay Cross in August 1944 and on our first date we went to the Park. It has many happy memories for me.* (Fenwick)

In 1941 unnecessary railings were requisitioned for scrap. The Parks and Cemeteries Committee resolved that most of the railings in and around the Park had to be retained for safety purposes. Amongst the railings removed were those around the cricket ground; unfortunately this meant that people began using it as a short cut and considerable damage was caused. The parks superintendent was authorised to purchase some chestnut palings as a barrier. Then a letter came from Emergency Works Officer to the Ministry of Works and Planning saying that the gates and railings around the Park appeared to fall outside the exempted categories and must go for scrap; those round the Annexe could be retained as that was military property. The committee did not approve of their removal and the town clerk was instructed to 'make representations to the Ministry for their retention'. The Emergency Works Officer replied that in view of the Council's objections the railings could be retained until the situation deteriorated. Fortunately it never did and the railings remained.

As well as losing their railings, many public parks and recreation grounds were partly dug up to provide allotments for the 'Dig for Victory' campaign. Queen's Park escaped this fate although the conservatory was used for growing tomatoes.

By 1942 the restrictions on travel and the lack of accommodation at holiday resorts meant that most people had to spend their holidays at home. The Ministry of Labour and National Service requested councils to provide recreation and entertainment and the 'Holidays at Home' movement began. An ambitious programme of events was organised, many of them taking place in the Park. These continued until after the war but in 1945 it was renamed the 'Summer Entertainments Programme'.

Dr Goodfellow, who lived at the junction of Foljambe Avenue and Walton Road, devised his famous 'iodine tablet'. These were hung in trees around the Park, also in C.B.C. Transport buses and in various schools in the borough. It was supposed to give the populace the seaside aroma. If it did I do not know, but it gave us a fillip. Thomas Redihough, who was the parks foreman, was in charge of putting these tablets in various parts of the Park etc. Unfortunately with him intimately handling these iodine tablets, he got iodine poisoning; it nearly killed him. He was gravely ill in Chesterfield Royal Hospital for quite some time but he eventually recovered. (Silcock)

On the field near the bandstand you could have a ride on a donkey or horse or have a ride in a pony and trap, you had to pay. (Maycock)

In the summer time we had the donkey rides, along with a little cart for the younger ones. They were wonderful. During the evening

The donkeys were a popular feature of the 'Holidays at Home' events. (Chesterfield Museum)

from my bedroom window I just had to watch them returning from the Park along Dixon's Road, before I would settle myself down for the night, happy to know that they also were going to rest for the night in their field, ready for the next day in the Park. (Southern)

I looked after the donkeys in 1944 and 1945. Two years was enough. (Goodyear)

During the summer months Mr Sykes and Mrs Sykes and their children, Elaine and Jack, used to bring their amusement fair, swinging boats, slot machines, roundabout, roll-a-penny stall. They had a beautiful gypsy-type caravan and the fair stood on the grass by the house, which now has the bridge by it, replacing the lawn tennis courts. (Maycock)

We had double summer time and in June it did not really go dark, which caused all sorts of problems for parents as children did not want to go to bed. Anyway on this evening (Friday) in midsummer I had been to the Scouts and on the way home stopped at the fish and chip shop adjacent to the Royal Oak along with the rest of the troop. We enjoyed our meal and proceeded into the Park. We eventually arrived at Sykes Amusements and one of our gang suggested we employed 2d. or 3d. on a swing boat ride so we all piled on. What a disaster; the stomach and digestive system could not cope with the rocking and swinging of the boat on top of a recently devoured bag of fish and chips. I cried: 'Stop the boat'. Mr Sykes applied the brake. I jumped off and ran to the cricket field where I was violently sick. When I eventually arrived home I did not dare tell my parents. When my mother enquired if I wanted any supper, I declined the offer, saying that we had a busy time at Scouts, and went to bed. Never again will I eat fish and chips and take a swing boat ride. (Silcock)

American troops stationed nearby demonstrated how baseball was played. It was interesting to find that baseball proceeds at the same pace as cricket and when a match was broadcast by a local station on the radio I found it quite easy to follow the play. Maybe we should have carried on playing baseball after the war, youngsters would have enjoyed it, being a cross between rounders and cricket and, who knows, we could have played and even beat the Yanks. (Cockell)

During the war, possibly 1944, a jamboree was held in the Park for scouts from all over the county. They set up camp sites etc. It was quite an occasion. 25th Chesterfield (Saltergate Meths), of which I

40

was a founder member, had a patch near the bandstand. 1st Tapton House Troop had a post just opposite the conservatory. Also allowed to attend, although not scouting, were the Woodcraft Folk, the Co-op's attempt to emulate the scouting movement. Three big parades spring to mind. Lady Baden Powell, the widow of Lord Baden Powell, founder and former World Chief Scout, came and inspected the assembled Girl Guides on the cricket ground. She took the salute on a raised dais on the tarmac cycle track opposite the pavilion. In similar circumstances Lady Edwina Mountbatten, Commandant of the St John's Ambulance Corps, did the same. After her inspection she addressed them on their fine turn out and took the salute.

Another big occasion, possibly 1942, was the visit of the Princess Royal. My late dad, being a sergeant in the C.B.C. Rescue party based in the Borough Engineer's Department, had to arrange the rescue of an injured civilian from the top floor of the cricket pavilion. They had to make out it had been blitzed etc. They were rehearsing for a couple of weeks beforehand. Anyway on the day of the inspection it was fine and dry. Mother and I were awarded VIP seats in the pavilion. What an honour. Anyway my Dad did fine and the exercise went very well, the body was lowered out of the pavilion and loaded into an ambulance. The Princess Royal thanked all the personnel involved and thanked my father for the fine effort

The Princess Royal visited the Park on more than one occasion. Here she inspects the Home Guard in 1941. (Chesterfield Museum)

and performance. She inspected all the Home Guard Companies from around the Chesterfield area and took the salute. The C.O. for the day was Major Dan Newton.

In July and August each year on a Sunday all the top brass bands entertained the Park audiences; Brighouse and Rastrick, Fairey Aviation, Manchester C.W.S., Grimesthorpe Colliery, who had their own East Midland Bus with a portion on the top for their instruments, and finally the best of the lot the Foden Motor Works Band with their conductor Harry Mortimer. The concerts used to start at 3.00p.m. 'til about 4.30p.m. – 4.45p.m. and resume after tea. Entrance into the bandstand arena within the privet hedge was 3d. with a programme for 1d. A small wooden shed was the admission office. The audience sat on wooden slats in iron frame mouldings. We could never afford the entrance so had to listen on the grass, weather permitting. The bandstand had a circular sliding glass partition to allow for bad weather, so even if it was raining, the concert took place. It must have cost the C.B.C. a lot of money to put on these concerts. (Silcock)

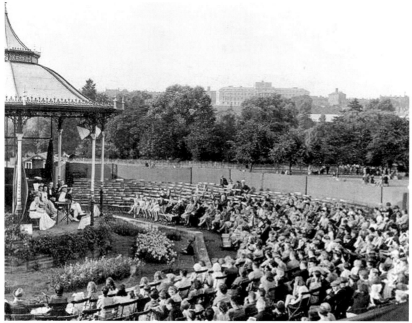

A play reading at the bandstand, the sliding partition can just be seen on the left. (Chesterfield Museum)

42

We had Ralph and Ernest Hopkinson working with us and Ralph's father-in-law, whose nickname was Pot and Pan. We had to paint a white line so that the chairs could be set out in a straight line. One day Tindale was there — he always had a cigar on. He shouted to Pot and Pan to come and paint a line where his feet were. Pot and Pan painted straight over his shoes. Never forgot it! (Goodyear)

Concert parties were housed in a large marquee, near the bandstand on public holidays. (Wilbourne)

Every Sunday and at holiday time there were concerts and plays, also brass bands. (Maycock)

We had to bring the piano from Hasland on the back of a lorry. A bloke called Bill Pashley would play the piano all the way back to Queen's Park. (Goodyear)

Later on in the war a big sports meeting was held each year with athletics and Cumberland wrestling. Chief Constable Milner was the prime mover of these events. (Wilbourne)

Also at this time the Chesterfield Borough Council introduced the Municipal Sports usually on a Saturday at the end of June. It was a very good day of pleasure with the usual track and field events and Cumberland wrestling. Lots of guest runners and local celebrities etc. (Silcock)

To celebrate the return of peace in July 1946 the Maternity and Welfare Committee held a garden party and gala in the Park. There was a flower and vegetable show, children's fancy dress parade, mothercraft and fathercraft competitions as well as Miss Parry's troupe of performing alsatians and James Wakefield, conjuror and ventriloquist.

A Changing World, 1946-99

The post-war years marked a turning point for the Park. Its use to stage big events declined. The establishment of the National Health Service in 1948 meant that there was no further need for fund raising events for the hospital. By 1951 people were again able to go away for their holidays. The organisers of the Festival of Britain Show on 4 August reported that the attendance was 'not encouraging'. They thought that this was because half the town was on holiday as many of the works were closed. All thoughts of reviving the Chesterfield Carnival were abandoned. 1951 was also the last year for the much loved Sykes amusements. A year later the Parks Superintendent had another use for the land they occupied.

The Municipal Sports continued.

I think it was 1949 that Macdonald Bailey, the famous Wembley 1948 Olympic Sprinter, ran in the 100 and 220 yards, winning easily. (Silcock)

I used to run the last leg in the relay for William Rhodes. The master, Harry Husband, used to take us to the Park to practice. On one occasion Macdonald Bailey was running round the Park. Suddenly he opened up his stride, and his long legs ate up the ground, a sight I have never forgotten. (Sowden)

I remember the athletics meetings there used to be when I was young (about 55 years ago). It was quite an event for me as my Dad would take me and we had a programme and marked every race result. I particularly remember the cycle racing — somewhat different to the ones in the Olympics, it was each rider for his or herself around the tarmac track. Names like Beryl Burton come to mind. Also the 'walking' races were quite fascinating to watch. I was really pleased a couple of years ago to meet Roland Hardy, who was the Chesterfield area star at this race, when we were playing in a Crown Green Bowling Match at Highfield and he was there. I still have his autograph from those days. (Baskerville)

The bicycle races on the cycle track around the cricket field were great, we loved it when our champion Roy Stubbs was racing for what we called the Spireites racing team, how we loved to cheer him on to win. (Southern)

The standard of local athletics was high. Taking part in the second annual championships of the Chesterfield Harriers and Athletic

Municipal Annual Athletic Sports (Open).

(WET OR FINE). Under A.A.A., W.A.A.A. and N.C.U. Laws.

SATURDAY, JUNE 17th, 1950, 2-30 p.m.   QUEEN'S PARK, CHESTERFIELD.

Chesterfield Municipal Ninth Annual Sports will again introduce to the sporting audience many athletes of world-wide repute, the programme will be continuous from 2-30 to 5-30 p.m. Additional events which will cater for Championships have been included, and everyone can be assured of excellent performances by world-renowned athletes.

The chief events will be:—

SIX MILES CHAMPIONSHIP of the Northern Counties A.A. The foremost long-distance runners in the North will compete including Dr. Aarons (National Cross-Country Champion, 1949 and 1950), W. Hesketh (Holder, and Junior Cross Country Champion), G. Saunders, Birch and other Internationals).

100 YARDS NORTHERN COUNTIES JUNIOR WOMEN'S CHAMPIONSHIP.

CYCLE CHAMPIONSHIP.

GREAT ATHLETICS MATCH. Champions representing Yorkshire, Cheshire, Notts., Derbyshire, Leicestershire and Lincolnshire will contest TEN events:— 100 yds., 220 yds., 440 yds., 880 yds., Mile. Hurdles, Javelin, Discus, Pole Vault, Relay Race.

It is anticipated that the following will compete:—
L. Eyre—Empire One Mile Champion and Northern Record Holder.
B. Shenton—Empire Games Sprinter and Northern Champion.
C. T. White—Empire Games Runner and Olympic Competitor.
J. Archer—European Sprint Champion, Empire and Olympic Games Team Captain.
Also 29 County or Area Champions, Internationals and Olympic Athletes.

Plaques will be presented to the first three at Victory Ceremonies.

ALL GATES OPEN 1-0 P.M.

ADMISSION TO PARK: Adults 1/-, Children 6d. Payable at Gate. Transfers to East Wing Enclosure, 1/- (no half-price). Payable at Stand.

WEST ENCLOSURE BOOKING.—You may book seats BEFORE the day of the Sports for this Enclosure which will hold 600. Tickets which will admit you to the Park and ensure that you get a seat (not numbered) in this Stand may be obtained by forwarding Cash, P.O., etc., together with stamped addressed envelope for return of ticket, not later than June 15th, to the Hon. Secretary, E. R. L. POWELL, Denewood, St. John's Road, Chesterfield.

Tickets (including Tax), 3/- each.

OPEN EVENTS. ALL SCRATCH.

100 Yards Flat Race	1st Prize—value £5/5/-
220 Yards Flat Race	2nd Prize—value £3/3/-
880 Yards Flat Race	3rd Prize—value £2/2/-
One Mile Flat Race	Plus Plaques for 1st, 2nd, 3rd.
440 Yards Cycle Race	1st Prize—value £5/5/-
1,000 Metres Cycle Race	2nd Prize—value £3/3/-
	3rd Prize—value £2/2/-
	Plus Plaques for 1st, 2nd, 3rd.

JUNIORS (under 19 years of age on June 17th, 1950)—

100 Yards Flat Race	1st Prize—value £3/3/-
One Mile Flat Race	2nd Prize—value £2/2/-
	3rd Prize—a Plaque.
	Plus Plaques for 1st and 2nd.

WOMEN (over 15 years of age and under 18 years of age on June 17th, 1950)—

100 Yards Flat Race	1st Prize—value £3/3/-
	2nd Prize—value £2/2/-
	3rd Prize—Plaque.
	Plus Plaques for 1st and 2nd.

BOYS (over 10 and under 15 years of age on June 17th, 1950)—
100 Yards Flat Race (over 10 and under 13 years of age).
Plaques for first three.
100 Yards Flat Race (over 12 and under 15 years of age).
P'aques for first three.

GIRLS (over 10 and under 15 years of age on June 17th, 1950)—
100 Yards Flat Race (over 10 and under 13 years of age).
Plaques for first three.
100 Yards Flat Race (over 12 and under 15 years of age).
Plaques for first three.

The Plaques awarded will be specially engraved with the Title, Coat of Arms, Date and Event and placing of the competitor, and will form lasting souvenirs of the winner's placing.

ENTRY FEES.
Senior Events—1/6d. for each events.
Cycling Events—1/6d. for one event, 2/6d. for two events.
Juniors and Women—1/- for each event. Boys & Girls, 6d. per entry.

ENTRIES CLOSE ON MONDAY, JUNE 12th (First post).

Entry Forms and details from the Hon. Secretary, E. R. L. POWELL, Denewood, St. John's Road, Chesterfield.

Among the guest athletes for the 1950 sports was Jeffrey Archer - Empire and Olympic Games team captain. (Chesterfield Museum)

Club, held in the Park in 1949, were Kathleen Stansfield, Betty Stone, Mavis Elcock and Margaret Gaughan. They had returned from the English Women's Junior and Intermediate championships with two trophies, one for the girls' relay race, the other for the junior girls team with most points. Mavis Elcock also won two individual titles. Also taking part in the club championship was local boy Ben Stoppard who beat Jeffery Archer (now Lord Archer) in the 100 yards in a later Municipal Sports.

In 1952 the Municipal Sports attracted 12,840 through the gate; a year later there were just 5,030, although the weather was regarded as ideal. The reason was thought to be the televising of the England v Australia test match. There was a deficit on the day of £220 1s. 4d. In November the honorary secretary and the honorary treasurer resigned and the 1954 sports were cancelled. This was a sad end to an event which had attracted high class athletes and cyclists for twelve years.

Also in 1953 plans for celebrating the Coronation were distinctly low key 'in view of the other activities to be held in Chesterfield on Coronation Day and the counter attraction of the TV broadcast of the coronation ceremony in London'. This was just as well as the fête was washed out by the rain.

45

The schools athletics championships, which began in 1931, continued.

The school sports days were held on the cricket pitch area. I can always remember how proud we all were at the end of the day when all the schools would march round to music to represent their schools. (Southern)

I ran for William Rhodes twice in the school sports. In the 220 yards in 1944, I came third, in 1945 second. That year I beat Al Needham of trumpet and jazz fame. He played for a bit in the Victoria band, i.e. Stan Cox. Al ran for Gilbert Heathcote, he came fourth. In 1945 Wilf Boon ran for William Rhodes and won the 440 yards in record time. He was tragically killed whilst studying at London University, playing rugby for them. He was only 19 at the time. Another fine athlete from William Rhodes at this time was Arthur Wain, later to be Mayor of Chesterfield about 1984 or 1985. (Silcock)

Band concerts remained popular after the war.

In the early 1950s following evensong in Chesterfield Parish Church, a number of young men from the church choir, together with their female companions from the congregation, would always proceed to the Park to hear the concluding items from the band concert on the bandstand. Sitting on the grass outside the fenced off area of course, you had to pay for a wooden seat within the enclosure. (Hallam)

During the mid to late 1950s I was a member of Staveley Military Band. Every summer we gave concerts in the Queen's Park Bandstand. On one notable Sunday the band arrived at the Park just as a very heavy rainstorm started. It soon became clear that the rain was in for the rest of the day and not many people would be visiting that evening; but then strange things began to happen. Firstly a message was received that the venue had been changed to Bradbury Hall. Consequently the band descended onto Bradbury Hall and set up the equipment for the usual 7p.m. start, but what about the audience? The second mystery of the day was that the hall gradually began to fill and we had a large audience for our concert. I never did find out how they all knew where to come. (Brown)

In the late 1950s the Council decided on economy: the budget for the bands was reduced, which meant that the leading bands no longer came. An additional sum was spent on dance bands at Whitsun and August Bank Holidays; they included names such as the Constant Flux Band and the Cliff Turner Dance Band.

Ernie Kay tends the hydrangeas in the conservatory. (Gaunt)

I remember in the 1960s the local pop groups of the day played in the bandstand on Bank Holiday Mondays. I can remember one band was called Steve White and the Zeroes. We all had a good time clapping and dancing. (Howarth)

I can remember people dancing on the grass. (Southern)

The horticultural displays remained a big attraction.

There was a bank of greenhouses behind the pavilion. When I began work in Queen's Park in 1943, I was the first bound apprentice employed by the Parks Department. I worked with Mr Ernie Kay who was the propagator. The plants for the Mayor's functions all came from Queen's Park. (Widdowson)

A popular feature in 1942 was the carpet bedding design for the 'Holidays at Home' scheme, on the slope opposite the conservatory.

We now move on to the famous badge. This was right opposite the conservatory. The badge was prepared and designed by Miss Cath Parry, head gardener at Tapton House. All the plants and flowers which were used in the design were grown at Tapton. Hours of work were put into its design and planting. People came from miles around to view it. Different themes were used — Boy Scouts, Girl

47

One of the popular carpet bedding displays. (Chesterfield Museum)

Guides, different anniversaries etc. One year the 'Aussie' team had their group photograph taken with the badge. This appeared in the local and national press. Now sadly two boulders rest there. (Silcock)

The plants came from Tapton nursery, where cuttings were taken every year. This was one of the jobs I did. I also did the designs which would take about six months to prepare and plant out, using between 4,000 and 8,000 plants depending upon the design. I remember doing one for the Rotary Club. The Derbyshire Times used to come every year and take photographs. The last time it was done was possibly 1985. (Billyeald)

The cricket matches too were exciting when the Australians came to play from Down Under. The head gardener, Mr Ernest Kay, made the Park gardens look nice, the Australian badge was always set out in plants by carpet bedding, a project that required much patience and skill to achieve, this I am sure would make the Australians feel very welcome in Chesterfield Queen's Park when they came to play cricket. (Southern)

Cricket matches remained as popular as ever. Matches against the old enemy, Yorkshire, were always keenly awaited.

One of my most enjoyable memories of the Park was my first coun-ty cricket match on a June Saturday in 1948, Derbyshire v Yorkshire was the game and what a day's cricket we had. My pals and I arrived at the Park Road entrance to find things very busy, in fact we missed the toss and the first two wickets to go down, the queues were so long, the gate turned out to be 14,000, a ground record. George Pope was unplayable that day. After the match, so Derbyshire folk-lore tells us, George told Norman Yardley, Yorkshire and England captain at the time, to put that in his pipe and smoke it! George's swipe, so we are told, was due to the fact that he had been called into the England squad for the test match at Trent Bridge (?) but was then made 12th man. George took umbrage at this and returned to play for his county, saying there was more to his talents than being a waiter, a reference to taking the drinks out. (Cole)

Yorkshire won the toss and decided to bat. Herbert Halliday and Ted Lester opened the batting and Halliday took first strike. He wasn't satisfied with the position of the sight screen at the lake end. It had to be moved and also the spectators, hell to play. Still not satisfied, more hell to play. All this time the late great George Pope had the new ball in his hand, passing it one to the other, waiting patiently. Eventually Halliday was satisfied. The umpire called 'Play' and the first ball from George shattered Halliday's stumps all over the place.

Chesterfield Cricket Club in August 1947. (Lowe)

49

The ground erupted. By lunch Yorkshire were all out for 44, includ-
ing the captain Brian Sellers. Derbyshire went in after lunch and
scored 277. So Yorkshire had to go in for 45 minutes and bang
George did it again and by stumps Yorkshire were 19 for 3. A great
victory was in sight on Monday, but what happened, it rained all
day. Tuesday wasn't much better. Yorkshire wouldn't come out to
play. Spectators threw cushions at the Yorkshire dressing room.
Play eventually resumed, and at 6.30p.m. Yorkshire were 37 for 6
and the match was drawn. What a dream it would have been if
Derbyshire could have beaten a team of England players.* (Silcock)

The Parks Department took over the preparation of the wicket
and the organisation of the matches. To accommodate the large
crowds, temporary seating was installed on the cycle track.
Inevitably this led to a conflict of interests. As early as 1950 the
Chesterfield Cycling and Athletics Club complained about the lack of
facilities for cyclists and Chesterfield Harriers also sought improvements. In 1953 they asked that the Park Annexe be developed for
athletics because shot putt and javelin were not allowed on the
cricket ground. In 1956 there were no applications to use the cycle
track, which was out of use for long periods because of the temporary seating for the cricket. There was cycling on only a few occasions after that. In 1962 an athletics track was laid out in the Park
Annexe and the following year all athletics events were held there.

At first we used to keep taking the stands down. To make it easier,
we numbered each piece of wood. (Goodyear)

Also there was conflict because the Park was closed to the public during cricket matches.

The Queen's Park was closed for the six county cricket matches
played on the cricket field, so for 18 days each year notices were
posted on each of the three entrances each time to that effect. It
caused a bit of resentment and grumbling but people had to walk
round on these occasions. A kindly doorkeeper would let in a moth-
er with a pram or pushchair or possibly a 'babe in arms' but it did
not cause too much upset. Later on in the 60s and 70s it caused
quite a stir, the general public saying that it was their Park and why
should it be closed for these long periods. So the rules were relaxed
and fencing put along the side of the ground adjacent to the band-

* Although Yorkshire were without Hutton, Yardley and Coxon for this match, Derbyshire were without Townsend, Vaulkhard and Copson.

50

A band concert during the lunch interval of a county cricket match.

stand. But it was really a laugh because by this time the bridge had been placed over Markham Road and the general public could see without paying. (Silcock)

However, in the post-war years of austerity, the Council received a proportion of the gate receipts, and rental for the use of the ground, and the county club contributed to the cost of improvements to the pavilion.

At one point my friend and I got bored and went to the playground which I believe was situated near the swimming baths at the time. When we wanted to return to watch the cricket, the gateman would not let us back in — our tickets were with my friend's father. Luckily my friend and I managed to get past a different gateman who was manning the Boythorpe Avenue entrance and return to the match. (Franks)

When children got bored, they could always go for a swim. Unfortunately my son preferred a trip on the lake. I had never rowed a boat before and have never rowed one since! (Murphy)

And of course there was the famous beer tent!

Mansfield Brewery ran it for many years. On this occasion business was brisk when suddenly a violent thunderstorm occurred. A terrific wind got up which caused the tent to collapse. Len Slater who worked at the Sheffield Telegraph and Star, a printer on nights, always ran the bar during the cricket matches. The tent collapsed on him. He was very lucky, he was taken to the Royal Hospital and survived; others were shaken but not seriously injured. (Silcock)

Of the limited-over cricket matches one in particular stands out.

The most exciting one day match ever seen at Queen's Park was Derbyshire's victory over Sussex on 30 July 1969, a semi-final of the Gillette Cup. 10,582 spectators watched a famous victory over the masters of one-day cricket at that time. The day was fine but the pitch damp and Derbyshire struggled to what appeared to be a weak total of 136, sections of the crowd shouting their disapproval. However the Sussex innings began in a hushed atmosphere more like that of a match at the Crucible, as our two friends Rhodes and Ward steamed in. After 14 tense overs the usually flamboyant Martlets had scored only ten runs for two wickets. The roar at the end of each maiden over was deafening. The rotund, popular Fred Rumsey and the Hathersage-born Peter Eyre continued the fiery onslaught, man of the match Peter picking up six wickets as the Sussex men were humbled for just 49 runs. Hundreds inspected the straw-coloured wicket after the match and dwelled to savour the

The scene during the presentation after the Gillette Cup semi-final, somewhere there is a cricket pitch!

moment, though not with amber nectar as the beer tents had run dry early in the Sussex innings! We journeyed to the final at Lords, where Derbyshire lost a disappointing match to Yorkshire, but the memory of the semi-final victory matures like old port. (Hartley)

The spectators who watch Chesterfield Cricket Club may not be as numerous, but they still take a keen interest.

It was my first game as the new Chesterfield captain and I wanted to sparkle. It was not to be because after the first ball the score-board read 0-1. Five minutes later I was stalking round the Queen's Park ground after having been given out to a catch which bounced in front of first slip. My thunderous and ill-tempered walk took me past a group of old lads who used to sit on the right side of the pavil-ion and although they were staunch Chesterfield supporters, they never overlooked the chance to poke fun at our players — particu-larly the new captain out for a duck. Five minutes after a duck is never the time to speak to me and for that matter I'm not really in a cheerful humour five minutes after any end of innings. After play-ful banter between us — mine conducted through a forced smile and clenched teeth — one of them said: 'What's a ruddy Yorkshireman doing captaining Chesterfield anyway?' To which I answered: 'I'm doing missionary work trying to teach you Derbyshire Tups about fair play.' Thinking I'd won that round I turned in triumph to resume my walk only to hear someone to shout after me: 'Tha' might know about cricket, but tha's geography is no good — these boggers come from Nottinghamshire.' My grandfather always said that if you wanted a fool in Derbyshire, you had to take one with you, and he was right as these old lads constantly proved to me. (Baxter in *Chesterfield Cricket Club - 100 Not Out*)

The former Lancashire, Derbyshire & East Coast line closed in 1957 and the station and embankment were demolished. In their place were built the offices of the Accountant General's Department of the General Post Office and the Markham Road extension. A new footbridge from West Bars was opened in December 1963. Shortly afterwards the Council purchased the trackbed of the old Midland Railway branch and turned it into a cycle track and public right of way.

During the Second World War North Lodge became offices, was used as a dwelling once more from 1954, due to the post-war short-age of housing, and reverted to offices in 1968.

The Accountant General's Department of the Post Office towered above North Lodge for over 30 years. The main entrance is again from West Bars.

The Parks Superintendent used to have his office on the ground floor at the front. The secretary used to be upstairs. Also about this time electricity was laid on. (Ramskill)

Until I was nearly four we lived in Hasland. One day my mum left me outside a shop on Hasland Toll Bar whilst she made her purchases. I climbed out of my pushchair and carried on walking towards the town. When mum caught up with me she asked where I thought I was going. I replied: 'To see my daddy.' You see on fine afternoons my mum would take me to Queen's Park to see my father, Ken Bates, who was groundsman there. Everyone in the Park used to make a great fuss of me. My uncle Fred used to drive a van for Mellors who sold ice cream outside the Park Road and Boythorpe Road entrances. They made a cake from ice cream for my birthday. It was yellow, pink and green. (Gaunt)

Inside the Park refreshments were now available from a hut near the conservatory.

For many years it was run by Grosvenor. He knew everyone who worked in the Park and we could go along there in the afternoon and get a cup of tea and a bun or a cake. (Goodyear)

The paddling pool was closed in the early 1960s, initially because of the fears of the spread of poliomyelitis but also because of safety.

It was great fun at first, but after a while the bottom became very slippery with leaves and moss. There was many a wet weeping child taken home from there. The area was turned into a small garden for a while and then vanished completely when the small pool and walk were made at that end of the lake. (Booth)

We called it the Burma bridge because it was built with blood, sweat and tears. (Ramskill)

The much-loved children's playground was closed to make way for the swimming pool in 1967, and a smaller one opened alongside. In turn this was removed to make way for additional parking when the leisure centre was built round the swimming pool in the 1980s. Nationwide at this time there was a greater investment on indoor leisure facilities rather than outdoor recreation grounds. There was also a shortage of money and materials for major projects.

When I started in 1964 money was a bit tight and most of the staff only worked during part of the year. During the winter months they either went on the dole or were employed by other council departments. One year I painted the railings in the cattle market. (Ramskill)

The playground was moved to allow the construction of the swimming pool. The slide was reduced in height for safety reasons. (Chesterfield Museum)

55

The ranger with his dog was a reassuring sight.
(Chesterfield Museum)

A playground for juniors was opened in the south-west corner of the Park and one for young children in the corner between the cricket ground and the lake.

Growing up in Chesterfield I spent a lot of time in the Park. There was a junior playground. The piece of equipment I liked best was a little red roundabout for four people. We sat on a seat and held onto a bar on the top. We used our hands to make it go round as fast as we could. There was also a rocking horse, slide and swings. (Poulton)

The park keeper walking round with his dog was a deterrent to any anti-social behaviour. (Hoole)

An innovation in 1976 was the miniature railway.

We wanted to run it from Boythorpe Road to Park Road so that anyone wanting to go through the Park could have a nice ride on the train, but it was too easy for people to drop things off the footbridge onto the track. Instead it ran from the station to the footbridge and back but that wasn't very far and it was a bit boring. To make the ride more interesting, the track was relaid round the lake, and at the same time railings were placed around the lake for safety reasons. (Ramskill)

56

The problem was when we started laying it, there was a lot of rain and it was just like digging porridge — it all had to be dug by hand. What people don't realise was that it was meant to go the other way round. Also the engine kept jumping off the track, usually when people were on the train. We even had bars fitted across the bottom of the engine so that it could be lifted back. In the end they decided to buy a stronger model which is the one they've got now. (Goodyear)

As well as cricket matches, there were other televised events in the Park.

Progammes like Multicoloured Swap Shop and cricket matches took a couple of days to set up and were cleared away straight afterwards. We liked them though because the television companies paid us extra for jobs like laying cables. Game for a Laugh was filmed mostly in the swimming pool. The programme with Thora Hird lasted about three months. She had to climb over a gate and ladder her stockings. She had a ride on a boat and went into town to get some new tights. Thora Hird was a real lady, she used to have tea with us in the mess room. (Ramskill)

BBC Television had a children's programme called Multicoloured Swap Shop *which went out live on Saturday mornings and was pre-*

Roy Goodyear waves the flag, Councillor Whyatt takes the controls and, in the background, Frank Ramskill looks on. (Chesterfield Museum)

Colin Marsh (no7) in a snow-covered Park for Multicoloured Swap Shop. (Marsh)

sented by Keith Chegwin. The Chesterfield Motor Cycle Club was asked to arrange for some of the young riders from the scramble section of the club to take their motor cycles along to Queen's Park to demonstrate some scrambling techniques. One of the four boys who rode was my son Colin. On the day of the demonstration, the ground was covered with snow but they performed various manoeuvres and wheelies. When the demonstration was over, Keith Chegwin spoke to the boys and thanked them for giving their time and expertise to the programme. (Marsh)

There were other cameras in the Park.

We were married at the Registry Office in March 1975. It was a lovely sunny day, so we walked down to the Park to have our wedding photographs taken. (Smith)

The bedding displays in the Park were attractive but expensive.

We had students from Broomhill College to do some work in the conservatory. They built a rockery in the middle with a pool with goldfish in it. At one end of the conservatory there was a bed with cacti in it, at the other end, a sub-tropical area. (Pashley)

The early 1990s brought big changes. The adoption of Compulsory Competitive Tendering meant the Parks department no longer undertook

The low maintenance display established by students from Broomhill College.
(Chesterfield Photographic Society)

grounds maintenance. The glasshouses in the Park and at Tapton were closed and demolished, the carpet bedding scheme was abandoned, and South Lodge became offices. Maintenance was undertaken by external contractors.

However, if the Council thought that people no longer cared about the Park they were wrong. When the Council announced in 1989 that they proposed to demolish the bandstand, saying that the 'halcyon days of Sunday afternoon concerts were over', there was a furious protest. A public enquiry was held which found that the bandstand should be restored.

A year later the Council wanted to build an office block in the Park Annexe. There were more protests. However, E.G. Maynard, vendor of the land upon which both the Park and the Annexe stand, had imposed restrictive covenants on the sale, stating that the land was for the people of Chesterfield for ever and that it could not be sold for development, and the scheme was abandoned.

Several factors contributed to the demise of first class cricket in the park: the decision of the County Cricket Club to concentrate its resources at the County Ground at Derby, the changing structure of the game, particularly the reduction in the number of days played per season, and the increasingly outdated facilities. In 1998, almost immediately after a dinner to celebrate the centenary of first class cricket in the Park, the club announced that they would no longer play at Chesterfield.

Increasingly there was an air of under-investment in the Park: the herbaceous border became weed infested, the children's playgrounds lacked stimulation, the conservatory was closed because of its dilapidated state, the cricket facilities deteriorated, and catering facilities were basic. The cost of restoration was too high for the council alone.

The bandstand, without the decorative iron work on the canopy, before restoration in 1991.

A very sad sight — the dilapidated and weed infested conservatory prior to restoration.

2000: A New Beginning

The establishment of the Heritage Lottery Fund gave a lifeline to public parks in general. The first step was the application for listed status by English Heritage and the Park was designated Grade II in 2001. The consultants were chosen and, following extensive consultation with the public, a report was drawn up proposing that the early features of the Park should be conserved, and that the historic buildings in the Park should be refurbished for community use. The views across the grassy open space were to be restored and vehicular traffic in the Park reduced. Play facilities were to be upgraded and catering facilities and security improved. An application for lottery funding was made, which was successful in 2003.

Work on the restoration began on 16 February 2004. It was decided not to close the Park whilst the work was going on, which had the advantage that members of the public could see what was happening, although some pathways were closed to allow for the construction of two new main drains.

Progress was hampered by bad weather, including storms in July and August, one of which flooded the area around North Lodge.

The neglected herbaceous border has gone, the café is boarded up, but the view across the Park is back.

62

There were other problems.

The first problem came when we discovered that North Lodge had no foundations, having been built on a raft on the alluvial soil of a river bed. The new extension had to be built on piles. Unfortunately there was an old electric cable not shown on the plans and, when it was hit during piling, powers supplies to the Sports Centre and the Ravenside retail development were cut off! The silt from the lake was analysed repeatedly. Unfortunately one analysis showed the presence of residues washed into the lake from the industries of Brampton; the silt could not be returned to land and instead had to be deposited at the end of the lake. When work started on the conservatory, it was found that the front was beginning to sink, effectively pulling the building over. It was no mean feat to take the building apart piece by piece; 60 per cent of the wood had to be replaced. Painting took an age. The shelter too was on the verge of collapse. When the protective tinplate was removed from the central post, the wood was found to be almost completely rotten. The roof covering was not tiles, merely roofing felt treated to look like tiles. The internal timbers had all been made individually and were not standard sizes; most needed to be replaced. (Ramsey)

The pavilion was completed in time for a belated start to the cricket season. Derbyshire County Cricket Club returned in June for two practice matches in glorious weather and in front of big crowds. In July it was the turn of the children to enjoy a family fun day with the recently opened playground for young children in great demand. The sun also shone in September when Prince Edward made a tour of inspection and met people involved in the restoration work.

Generations of children have happy memories of Queen's Park.

As a child I lived at New Whittington, so Brearley Park was closer for us. My grandmother did take me to Queen's Park very occasionally, so it was more of an adventure. I particularly remember the walk down Wheeldon Lane, which was fascinating to me, going up and down the steps and along a secret alley (or so I thought), and then there was this amazing park at the end — the real stuff of childhood. (Knowles)

Queen's Park played a big part in my life during my childhood. We lived just off Hollis Lane and hardly a week would pass by without a visit there. It was always for me a wonderful place to go because there was always plenty to see and do. (Southern)

I spent many happy hours there as I lived across the road. (Booth)

They return, bringing their children and grandchildren.

In later years, married and exiled to the flat lands of Peterborough, I used to jump at any opportunity to bring our children to the Park. First would be the visit to the little statue of my mother, their grandmother, overlooking the cricket pitch, then ball games on the large expanse of green, fun on the swings and time to feed the ducks. None of us can recall the little train from those days but, after we had all moved homewards to Mansfield and the children married and gave us grandchildren, the trips to the Park included rides on the train and memories of my own childhood trips returned to be shared with this new generation. The visit to the statue and the exploration of the summerhouse jutting into the lake were 'must dos' as was of course the buying of ice cream and lollies from the booth. (Bell)

I would take my grandchildren to the Park. They are all grown up but I still go to the Park. (Maycock)

At the present time it's my three grandsons who are playing cricket in the Park. (Baskerville)

Long may it continue

The new toddler's play area. (Poulton)